Beauty born of pain

OKANAGAN
PUBLISHING HOUSE

a collection of poems by

Sally Quon

Formatting and layout by Jadon Dick

Published by:

www.OkanaganPublishingHouse.ca

Okanagan Publishing House is an imprint of

Okanagan Publishing Inc.
1024 Lone Pine Court
Kelowna, BC V1P 1M7
www.okanaganpublishinghouse.ca

Printed in the United States of America

1st Edition, March 2023

10 9 8 7 6 5 4 3 2 1

ISBN: 978-1-990389-30-6

Library and Archives Canada Cataloguing in Publication

Title: Beauty, born of pain / a collection of poems by Sally Quon.Names: Quon, Sally, author. Description: Includes bibliographical references. Identifiers: Canadiana (print) 20230185843 ·| Canadiana (ebook) 20230185851 | ISBN 9781990389306 (softcover) | ISBN 9781990389313 (EPUB) Subjects: LCGFT: Poetry. Classification: LCC PS8633.U66 B43 2023 | DDC C811/.6—dc23

CONTENTS

part two: **ECHOES**

part three: **DAMAGE**

part four: **RECOVERY**

Once Upon a Time

once upon a time
I was young –

beautiful, even.

until one day the big, bad wolf
swallowed me whole.

in the dark cavern of his
appetites,
I stayed
an eternity

waiting.

the huntsman
never came.

part one:

SECRETS

Have You Forgotten

promises made?
You stroked my hair
silken on the pillow, and we
laughed and cried and called out
to know each other's secrets
laying waste to the night
baring our shame for in
truth there is knowing,
forgiveness, and trust.
It's in the daylight
dreaming ends.
It's in the daylight
shadows form and
promises
are forgotten

Poetry by Sally Quon

Sorry, Not Sorry

I'm sorry
but I don't think I have
anything
to apologize for.
It was you
who raised your hand,
a surprise in the night
so often I stopped sleeping
naked, because
it made me more vulnerable.
It was you
whose tongue cut, with
edges like slips of shale,
the bite of a whip,
bringing me to my knees.
It was you
who undermined every move,
countered every effort,
like a strategic game of Risk

you didn't need to win
as long as I was the loser.

Broken

You took me –
raw and fresh –
wore me down,
broke me open.

You taught me lessons.

Taught them again
when it didn't work the first time.

You molded me
into the person I am today.
Look at me now.

Look, I said.

Are you proud of your work?

The Darkest Hour

The darkest hour
was not the one
before the dawn.

It was not the one that
cried
on a moonless night
in late November.

The darkest hour
came the day
the children were
taken
and instead of
comfort
you offered only silence and

left me alone
in the stone

cold shadows.

Case of Mistaken Identity

I'm not the one who hit my wife.
I'm not the one who terrorized my children.
I'm not the one who brought family services
down upon our heads.

I'm not the one who refused visitation,
quit on my family.
I'm not the one who made it all about me.

I'm not the one who accused everyone and remained blameless,
who wasted the money,
who called the names,
who laughed at the tears,

who drew first blood.

Didn't happen.

Wasn't me.

Walking Lightly

never knowing
rules of the game
every step
a misstep
every word
a challenge, leading to a fight
fractious love—contentious
better left behind

Poetry by Sally Quon

Reflection

the air is heavy
still
no wind to

whisper

through the grass
no leaves
dancing

in the trees
no birdsong to break the
silence

the feeders stand empty

all that is left is disappointment – a

reflection

in the glass

Just Thinking

Wouldn't it be nice
if I could just
close my eyes,

sleep away the pain?

Sometimes I lay in the dark.
Sometimes I toss and I turn –
sometimes I cry.

Every so often
I take a pill,
and every so often

I think about taking more.

A Love Poem

Love?

What the fuck is that?
What do I know
about love?
The only "love" I've known
was pain,
bitterness
soul-wrenching
anguish,
madness, and
fear.
Love?
No thanks.

I'm good.

On Walking Away from Abuse

Deep within a dusty box of worn-out shoes and
hand-me-down dresses -
a one-eared, tired old rabbit, patches
of dingy grey fur clinging on,
bits of stuffing
tumbling free.

Set aside to be discarded
until the child found it, claimed it,
christened it Bunny.

She wrapped it in a hug, swore to never
let go.

Fifty years later, she left it behind.

She had to let go.

Poetry by Sally Quon

Scars

I run my fingertips
over the landscape of my face.
Skin, no longer smooth.

The little chip
from the time he broke my cheekbone.
The scar above my eyebrow.
The shape of my mouth,

now that the teeth are gone.

He left his mark, alright.

I run my fingertips
over the landscape
of my face,
craving a touch
tender-blue,
feather light.

His Arms

The last time
he held me in his arms,
I cried.

I'd forgotten what it was like
to be touched.

To be touched -
skin to skin -
breathing his warmth,
feeling his strength.

Feeling as though he had my back,
he was on my side,

he loved me.

Unrealized dreams,
chimera of the heart.

Too much time alone,
adrift;
party of one.

Seeds of hatred
already sown between us.

Still,
I cried.

Pieces

Unexpected
pieces long forgotten
rise like the Western Anemone from spring snow
blossom brief

disappear, as suddenly as they came

A blink
        A yawn
                A momentary distraction

Pieces fall to the floor
crushed underfoot

Questions

great blue heron standing alone
at the edge of the pond

i wish i could speak bird

i have a few questions, like

with all that big, blue sky
how do you find love?

does it get very lonely
with all that empty space?

but then again,
who am i to ask?

Still

Passing time, fading scars,
still
I wake in the night
hearing him call my name.

Fear shivers through me.

I am stern with myself.
Leave the past in the past.
Still
he lingers,
a living ghost,
a nightly haunting.

How many years
will it take
to erase the past,
living under his rule?
Still living in his shadow.

When Love Dies

and earth crumbles
skies shatter
water erupts
what is left?
pain for what was lost
sorrow for what will never be
tears, for broken wings

easier
to lock myself away
not that it matters—
who would notice?

embracing solitude
discovering self
learning to love
growing strong—

Beauty Born of Pain

these are my tasks

absolved of guilt
I test my broken wings

learn to fly

Poetry by Sally Quon

Freedom

freedom is singing while I cook
blending spices, creating delicate flavors
complex layers to tempt the palate
knowing it will be appreciated, enjoyed
not thrown against a wall
because it wasn't what he wanted

freedom is leaving my journal
lying open on a table – just like that!
knowing it won't be read
my own words
turned against me

freedom is going to bed at night
knowing I won't be startled awake
pulled out of bed by my hair
beaten, until all thoughts of

freedom

are ground beneath his boot

part two:

ECHOES

The Mirror

Razor-sharp
lines etched in skin,
drawing down.

Who is this face?

What happened to the one that came before?
Who laughed and sang,
who lived and loved?

Whose love was wasted.

No trace left –
stranger in her place.

Reflections turn to waves,
waves
wash out to sea.

Wash out
to sea.

Poetry by Sally Quon

Life caught in the cracks,
Tidepools, once rich with life,
choking, dying.

They say every wrinkle tells a story.

Listen closely –
the past is speaking.

My Father's Daughter

Born into a strange world
left on the doorstep of a house
with no windows
I see nothing.

I remember

warm hands
deep voice, powerful stride
laughter, bellowing out
the smell of his skin
the way that he danced

I broke his heart once
seeing him cry
broke me too

On the Farm

The smell of sweet decay
rises from the fallen leaves
and broken poplars
in late September.
Geese cackle noisily,
cowbells ring.
Inside, the smell of apple pies baking,
Uncle Hank's pipe.
There are biscuits on the table,
coffee served in chipped mugs -
real cream and cubes of sugar.
"Gather the eggs, would you dear?"

The Secret

The secret was
to be kept
at all costs.

The judge said
if he did it again
it would mean prison.

We wouldn't want
to break her heart
by sending him to prison,
would we?

Besides,
there was no real
harm done.

Just some tickling
in the night.

Don't tell your father.

It wasn't that bad.

Poetry by Sally Quon

Wild Horses

Blowing snow, waves, and drifts,
ribbons across the highway.
Vision obscured in dim headlights,
tar-black night.

He didn't see
the wild horses,

And I, six years old,
in the cool, dark back seat
remember…

scream of brakes,

spinning, spinning,

thump and shatter.

Powerful leg punctures windshield--
inches from my brother's head.

Beauty Born of Pain

In a nearby farmhouse
wrapped in blankets,
tears
still drying on my face,

I jump

at the sound
of gunshots in the dark.

Grandma's House

Grandma doesn't live there anymore—
moved in with Uncle Fred awhile
before being locked away

at the nursing home in town.

Her house,
abandoned before I was born,
sags,
sinking back into the earth.
Peeling wallpaper, loose boards,
broken glass, where windows used to be.

Exploring the ruins for
hidden treasure, a dangerous
child's game.

Two clay discs still hang on the wall—
bluebirds on canary yellow background,
rusty saw,
small wooden plaque proclaims Jesus

Never Fails.

I imagine her in her kitchen
stirring a pot of stew,
feeding the seven children,
the ones who lived.
Gray hair tightly bound—not a strand out of place,
all the love and loss in her life
unrecognizable in her stoic gaze.

Poetry by Sally Quon

Sharon

When we were young,
we swam in the beaver dam,
plucked leaches from each others backs.
You were fearless
and knew how to do things
like churning ice cream,
birthing kittens,
and making tomato sandwiches.
The coyotes at night didn't frighten you at all.
You were the leader
and I would follow
as we marched through fields of wheat,
down dusty dirt roads,
because we wanted to go to Grandma's house
and you knew the way.

Beauty Born of Pain

We played in the grain bins and hay lofts,
explored the old farmhouse,
searching for forgotten treasures
as it slowly sank into the earth.
And when we were thrown
from Uncle Hank's horse
you got back on, while I…
I was too afraid.

The Matriarch

She keeps the cheese whiz in a drawer
so it's always soft.
Better to spread
on fresh baked bread, served warm
from the pot-bellied stove.

Sometimes there is honey.

Water, hand-pumped at the kitchen sink,
steams in the kettle,
keeping wood fresh and moist.

She might be out
in the oversized garden
(peas on trellis,
raspberry brambles,
sunflowers
brushing the sky)

or in the barnyard,
scattering seed, gathering eggs--

Beauty Born of Pain

in the field
harvesting grain,
feeding cattle,
mending fences.

Evening, back in the kitchen,

family gathers at the old oak table,
laughing and arguing,
the way families who love
often do.

Glancing at the photo of her own mother,
old silver frame
atop the highboy,

her children,
her children's children,

she smiles.

Poetry by Sally Quon

Hunting Bear

I was reading a poem
by a Buddhist poet-monk
and then I wasn't.
I was, instead,
five years old,
standing on a path
of crushed cones and pine needles,
with my father.

The sulfuric scent of hot springs filled the air.

I close my eyes
I can feel the sun on my face
and my father's hand,
warm, holding mine.
Armed with a cork gun,
walking in silence.

Hunting bear.

The Great Chicken Plucking of 1974

vats of boiling water
all hands, on deck
young, inexperienced

terrified

steaming feathers pulled
plucked
pliers on pinions

gagging on the smell
blowtorch burnt
soot and shit

tears
burning on my cheeks,

years

before I could eat chicken

Eyes of a Child

I close my eyes and picture
places I once was -
the streets where I grew up,
the steps behind the church,
the woodpile
where my cigarettes were stashed.

Spaces between years
sanded down, repainted,
polished till they gleam.

Nothing remains
but a glimmer
of hope.

Somewhere out there
things are what they always were.
Another child's eyes
will widen to see
the mice nesting in the shed,
the perfect nook in the crab apple tree,

the brook that used to flow
behind Charley Shipley's house.

There was a game we used to play
- hidden treasure.
My sister and I would hide things,
each for the other to find.
Silver coins and bangles,
beads from our mother's chest.

I wonder if we found it all?
Or if something was forgotten,
left waiting all these years?
Can you imagine,

just for a minute,

to be a child
discovering long-lost treasure?
A Spanish bracelet, or
that worn-out exercise book

filled with my lost poems.

Poetry by Sally Quon

Tale of a Girl

Black-haired and wild,
she was
capricious
by nature.

Staying up all night,
words, tumbling
from our mouths
like water over rocks.

Midnight feasts and magic spells,
rituals of our own
invention,
binding us together.

(I still have the ring you gave me.
I wear it sometimes when I feel alone.)
Remember the time
we got caught shoplifting?

Beauty Born of Pain

Forbidden to see you again
was my first heartbreak.
A week later, punishment
rescinded
we ran to each other
in the rain, like lovers in
some old movie,
crying and talking,
holding hands and singing,

our world restored.

Whatever happened?
Those days are lost,
faded shadows in darkness.
Friends are hard to find,
harder to keep.

But I've never forgotten you,
or the smell
of strawberry lip gloss.

Poetry by Sally Quon

Primal Instinct

It was my job
to make sure there were adventures.

The girls would do whatever I suggested.

Skinny-dipping at the abandoned quarry.

Hot, prairie sun,
ice-cold water rising from the depths.

Tender young flesh exposed
to harsh UV rays,

stolen bottle of Dom
passed between floating mattresses.

When planes flew over-head we'd sit up,
waving our arms,
shouting

as if we'd be heard –
giddy with our own audacity.
Breasts,
small, medium and large,
flying like flags.

Free at last, free at last.

I, for one, would spread my legs,
let the sun enter me, and
imagine.

In Touch

I wonder
where you are now,
if you ever think of me
and remember.

Like the time we were caught
making love in the backseat
of your yellow, banana car

by a farmer
on a slow-moving tractor.
You laughed
when he gave you a thumbs up
while I hid my face
behind my hands.   Later

we drank hot chocolate

watching the snow fall
through the window
of the old café.

Listen

Echoing crack of hockey stick on puck,
thump of puck hitting boards.
Sharp shiver of sound,
skate blades scraping ice.
Crunch of boots on snow,
as heard through toque covered ears.
Low, electric hum
of rink lights overhead.
The subtle, subtle shatter
of breath
freezing in the air.

The Kiss

The sweet, cool breeze
brings with it the memory
of your kiss,
catching me off guard,
leaving me breathless,

carrying me deep

into the fragrant night

I Believe

in porch swings
and lemonade,
holding hands
and ferris wheels

I believe
in Sunday dinners
and cherry pie
summer vacations
and peas, fresh from the garden

I believe
in country roads
crickets at twilight
crocheted blankets
and hand-written postcards

I believe in pot-luck dinners
where no one
makes a quinoa salad
and children run riot
overflowing with laughter

Poetry by Sally Quon

By the Stream

We never did succeed
in damming the stream,
toiling for hours
under the hot sun,
moving boulders, piling rocks.

No reason—it was just something to do.

Retrieving our stream-chilled beer,
we sat on the gravel bed
cooled our feet,
watched water
surge over rocks--

a miniature waterfall
created
by our failed dam.

Slow dancing to the Eagles
in the back of the truck

as twilight fell.

Gold

Standing on the side of the road,
Barb, in her faded denim jacket,
sunlight glinting from the silver streaks in her hair
and the pale blue crush of her eyes.

Thumbs out,
picked up by father and son.
Silence, winter thick.

They might be killers for all I know.

She forces cheerful chatter.
I stare out the window at the ocean bleeding past,
wondering if our bodies will ever be found.

They dropped us at the dock,
drove off without a word
leaving us surprisingly
intact.

On the ferry to Denman Island,
we tossed bread to the gulls, played "remember when"

till anguish broke the surface,
words
tangled in our throats.

Barb had friends on the island –
he threw clay, she worked the loom.

I don't remember their names.

Dandelion wine and homegrown weed.
Sunlight through streaked windows,
dust motes in the air.
Burnished wood,
age-worn and warm.

That's what I remember.

The spinning wheel in the corner shone like gold.

I imagined
Rumpelstiltskin out in the barn
waiting for us to leave.

Photograph

In the photo, I am smiling,
sitting high on the rocks
after scaling the falls, recklessly.

As if to say, "Watch me." Or
"I dare you,"
to my father-in-law.

The hike was his idea
and, inexperienced though I was,
I agreed to go.
My sneakers were new, blisters
rose quickly as he marched along.

I thought there would be pauses,
time to look, appreciate,
time to breathe.

Forests and streams flew by
at a relentless pace,
me, panting to catch up.

Fourteen miles later
we reached the base of the falls.
"Wow," he said, looking
up. "That's really something."

And he turned to go.

Dropping my pack,
I took my sore, screaming,
sneakered feet, walked into the water,
began to climb the falls.

I could hear him calling me back.
I wasn't listening. Slipping
on moss covered stones.
Cracking knees on boulders, icy
water numbing my hands.

I found a spot, sat down,
smiled fiercely—an act of defiance.

Screw you, Bob.

Water

i. Rain

Rain came – fell through the night. Whispers of moisture clinging to glass, one window stuck open – I don't know how to close it. That's what my life looks like. I went ahead and opened things, now I don't know how to close them. I dream about him sometimes. It's never good. All that anger. Years of anger, building up, never dissipating. I don't know if I even know what love is. I thought I did, but I was wrong. What if I had it once and didn't recognize it? What if I lost it before I knew it was there? I crave the feel of the coast, cusp of the world, watching the waves, feeling the pulse of the ocean drown out my heartbeat, blood in the vein. Touch – a jellyfish suspended in time.

ii. River

Remember the Ashnola River last June? It was so loud in our tent I couldn't sleep and when I did drift off, the river wound its way into my dreams. I'm not used to so much noise. It keeps me from thinking. But then, maybe that's a good thing. I spend too much time thinking, anyway.

This creek flows into the Similkameen, just like the Ashnola. And it's just as loud. I close my eyes--everything else disappears. Eventually, I suppose, you would get used to it, like an exhaust fan you don't hear until someone turns it off. In the silence your ears ring.

I can't hear any noise from the highway. It really is like the rest of the world has been shut off and there is only me, sitting at the base of the waterfall, alone with the American Dippers as they bob and dive.

iii. Lake

As water closed over my head, I could feel panic bubbling in my chest. Those internal voices were mocking me, telling me how ridiculous I was for getting into this situation., telling me I was an idiot that didn't deserve to live.

Darwin's Law and all.

I tried reasoning with myself, partly to fight the voices and partly to keep the panic from bursting out of me like the alien in the movie.

If I could stay calm, I could make my way to shore but the wrong parts of me were trying to float, keeping my head from reaching the surface. After everything I had been through in my life, was this how I was going to die? Ironic.

Never afraid of water. Always in control. An illusion, shattered by one windy day, one rogue wave. With a final, desperate push, my feet went down, and my head came up. Hands reached for me from the floating dock, pulled me up and laid me on sun-warmed wood. Eyes closed, I tried to regain control of my body, thrashing heartbeat, spattered breath.

I didn't see my rescuers. When I opened my eyes, I was alone. Maybe they weren't even real. Maybe it was Naitaka, spirit of the lake, the one white settlers called Ogopogo.

Poetry by Sally Quon

Kielbasa and Cabbage Rolls

My father used to say
"That's all we ate when I was a boy."
(kielbasa and cabbage rolls)

He would be so pleased
with this meal.
(perogies and potato salad)

Dinner for one, as if by preparing it
(sweet red cabbage, smoky bacon)
I could invoke his presence.
(ham and barley soup)

So I could tell him,
(potato pancakes)
so I could say,
(sauerkraut)

Daddy, I miss you.
(Silk Tassel)

Daddy, I made mistakes.
(Five Star Whiskey)
(Lonesome Charlie)
(Silent Sam and Pilsner)

Daddy, I'm all alone.

Poetry by Sally Quon

part three:

DAMAGE

Alone

She peers into the cedar tree, hearing magpie call,
impending rain, aching in her fingers.

Won't be long now.

A plate of sliced strawberries and devilled eggs
lies forgotten
on a table by the window.
Coffee, turning cold.

Humming a tune from a song of long ago,
singing of longing, hunger, and loss,
she pauses, pen poised over notebook.
Distracted by pain more intense,
less precise.
Distracted by stillness,
by the unwitting unveiling
of her eyes.

How did it happen?

Beauty and sorrow, both
spellbinding and repulsive,
capture light, throw it back
at hollow places,

absorbed

in the shadow of her solitude.

Doing Well

We went in search of wild horses,
driving through miles of watery valley,
fierce autumn colours
a momentary distraction.

I guess you could say
I'm doing well,
an all-purpose coating
of lies and conjecture,
designed to keep
chaos from escaping.
Negating the need to reveal,
lay open the dark
where light might pierce,
where admission demands action.

Until we found the wild horses

and everything changed.

Pale

I dreamed of a tangled garden,
Western Bluebirds and clouds of Swallowtails
under a silver sky.

In the cool grey shadows,
amid the cracked tiles
of a fallen cottage,
I dance on broken glass,
shattered dreams
reduced to sand.

Cobwebs

i.

Coming from a place of half-sleep,
half-dream,
voices in my head
tumble
far from above and again.
Slipping into the background,
shaking a new perspective
out of the haze.

Trying to remember
where we used to get that pizza.
How to find the fuse box…

…your name.

ii.

Living this way
colours, edges. A train
headed for the brink –
precarious and fragile.
Corners coming fast.
Ambient light, blind illusion.

Holding fast to the dream
beckoning from wild places,
I climb the stairs behind the billboard you can see
from the highway.

Overgrown with ivy,
one wrong move,
a turn of the ankle,
it crumbles to dust.

If only I could find you
before the clock runs out.

If only
I could find you.

iii.

Drifting in shadowy twilight,
slipping through cracks like a whisper,
misty traces of memory,
out of my grasp

and gone.

Evening Light

The light of the setting sun
filtering through the leaves and
blossoms on the trees,
filtering through the windowpane,
comes to rest upon my hand
like an age-spot
I am surprised
to see.

There Came a Moment

when what was closed
became open   truth
poured forth, unfiltered

met with silence

they don't know
how to handle my truth
and I
must learn to lie again

tempered

like glass

Speak Truth

fragile, tenuous
tomorrow
a rust-colored leaf, poised to fall
truth desensitized
unwilling to see
what does it mean?
stripped of deception
lies and omission
hope -
that final desperate act
precedes defeat

Inevitable

Sitting back, I watch
my body morph into something
unrecognizable
I am old
          oh, maybe not in years
but in painful memories

I have stretch marks on my tolerance
I have scars on my faith
There's a crack in my optimism

Time seeps in
spreads, poison-like
through spider veins

waves sweep me
perilous, toward dark--
surrender

Living Rough

He's been "living rough"
as they call it.
Skin over bones,
Frost-bitten hands.

"How're the kids?" he asks.
"They've got me quarantined -
top of the shelter.
Might have the virus.
Might not."

The words of the email blur and
rearrange themselves

"This is your fault.
You shouldn't have left.

I'm going to die; that's on you."

Beauty Born of Pain

I say nothing -
file the email
away with the others.

I've stood in front of this door before,
made the mistake of letting it open – a crack
was all he needed.

Suffered the pain inflicted
by frost-bitten hands

and a carcinogenic tongue.

Poetry by Sally Quon

Change

Winds shift branches,
sounds of change reach me
before the cool breeze touches my skin.

That's how it is sometimes,

the knowing.

Blink of eye, turn of head -
the intrepid conviction
of light's fast falling

even as darkness recedes.

The subtle way you know
promises don't matter,
lies are only lies
when someone else is telling them.
Truth
can't stand the light.

Beauty Born of Pain

Insoluble as death,
untenable as life,
constant.

Poetry by Sally Quon

Realistic

Most people dream at night
I wake up in the morning
make myself a cup of coffee
and dream

What's the good
of being realistic?
It doesn't make you happier,
it doesn't spare you pain

Give me the rose-colored glasses
the daydreams, the fantasies
Give me the gentle haze, the blissful ignorance
the lies

Let me go on believing
it's not so bad
it'll all work out
people are good

Beauty Born of Pain

And when I wake up
and the world is stark and cold
and there's nothing left to look forward to
and there's no one left to love
and I am alone…

…what then?

Poetry by Sally Quon

Wild and Precious Life

I plant my feet
stand firm, resolute
believe there is a way
to fix the broken
to find what I seek
            what was forsaken
            lost

clawing the earth
in search of buried treasure

pitted and dark
the holes I leave behind

Colour

I imagine my aura
ribbons of emerald green
cobalt blue and royal purple
ripple around my head

starbursts of stress-orange
angry-red
and sick-with-worry-yellow
assault the perimeter

keep me awake at night

Moonlight and Madness

touching thunder
vibrations
tumble free and
        drop
quiver and hold
shale-thin and jagged

path forged
through heart-hungry fen
desire and despair
lung-linked and pale
        calling my name
I hide in silence

Night

bits of darkness
cling to walls
heavy with hunger
reluctant egress

easy enough to be swallowed
into the hollow night
time slithers, belly-down
fear and pain
shriek in the black

whatever the night did bring
unseen
unheard
unremarked
as dawn pushes the dome of the sky

Pages and Pages

Yesterday suffocates
under pages and pages
of hastily scrawled words,
unresolved feelings,
half-remembered moments.

Today is about waking up,
relearning
to live and love,
to recognize
stardust, as it falls.

Then there's tomorrow –
full of unwritten stories,
winged dreams and shiny kingdoms.
Waiting for a crack in the concrete,
to push through,
to blossom.

Pearl

Just the soul scraped bare,
sensitive and raw,
I offer my truth to you;
await your judgement.

An oyster, broken open—
glistening flesh
exposed to light and air
shrivels and dies.

Hard truth remains,
a perfect sphere
of strength and hope.

Beauty, born of pain.

How to Remember You are Worthy of Love

Start by opening your eyes.
You can lay there a minute,
let the dawn wash over you,
until the need to pee forces you to rise.

Good.

Now that you're up, wash your face.
The shock of cold water will remind you you're alive.
Don't look in the mirror;
you don't need to see that.

Get yourself some breakfast, it doesn't have to be much.
Just enough to blunt the hunger.

Blunt

the hunger.

Beauty Born of Pain

Listen to the birds.
They always know what's what.
If you listen hard enough, eventually you'll understand.
That's what I keep telling myself, anyway.

Remember to drink lots of water--
it's important to stay hydrated.

I'm sorry,
what was I saying?

That Face

I look in the mirror
at the stranger I've become,
wondering,
how did this happen?

Scars
tell only part of the tale,
harder scars lie deeper,
far from sight.

Find one thing, I tell myself,
just one thing
to like.
Focus on that.

With dawn
new hope,
distance, forgiveness—

realization.

I am more
than that face in the mirror.

Cannot Forget

I wish I could say
happiness sticks
scattered and sunny

a dock for tomorrow
built
on pilings of love

no

I close my eyes
see his fist
violence and cruelty
blood and loss

try to forgive
cannot forget

Some Painful Truths

Here's one
I'm not very nice
I used to be
until life stripped
the skin from my back

I used to have compassion
until I was conned
I used to have empathy
until someone bled me dry
I used to be easygoing
until I was subjugated

What skin is left
hardened to a shell
an everlasting battle
holding on

Playground

On the playground
was a merry-go-round.
Flat wooden disk,

faded paint on weathered wood,
chipped paint and rust
on metal handlebars.

Grab a bar.
Run
run as fast as you can,
jump on, hold tight,

spinning and spinning.

Then a big kid with a wicked grin
would come along
spin the wheel,
secretly hoping to dislodge a kid or two.

Innocent fun is all.

Now, in this time of life,
the wheel spins faster and faster,
hands ache with the effort of hanging on,

grip slips away.

Bodies are flung off
to land in the grass,
stare at the sky,
disoriented and confused,
battered and bruised

waiting

for the spinning
to stop.

Small

insignificant, unimportant
almost not even here
and who would notice?
it doesn't matter
just another day
another way
of feeling

small

but when I open up
feel sun on my skin
wind in my hair

when the world towers over me
embraces and enfolds
I gulp wonder
the way a dying man gasps for air
even though I am small

like a cosmic puzzle

there is

still

a place for me

One Woman

standing on the
precipice
of feeling over form
enraptured
by a melody
eyes closed against the pain
the music painted colours that
blended
as she whirled
her sorrows fell away
… and she danced

Poetry by Sally Quon

Privilege

"The privilege of a lifetime is being who you are."

- Joseph Campbell

Sad,
to think I'd never be
the one who lived within.
You'd have liked her,
she was fun.

Breaking away
to newfound freedom,
she slowly emerges.
Older now, a bit less fun.

Celebrating life,
appreciating simple joy,
and grateful for the privilege.

Skies cloud over,
tides pull us under—life
gets in the way.
Sometimes, she needs a reminder.
Sand, between her toes.

All That I Am

I am a blade of grass underfoot
a drop of water, hanging from a web
a grain of sand, rolled by endless wave

I am a drop of blood, welling bright against pale skin

I am Rapunzel
          my body is the tower that holds me
I am the Little Mermaid
          voiceless and alone
I am Sleeping Beauty,
waiting
          to be woken

In Another Life, I Would Like to Be....

I used to think
I'd like to be a bird.
You know,
free as a bird and all that.

Birds aren't free.

Sure, they've got wings,
they can fly.
Compelled by instinct,
flying thousands of miles,
only to turn around, go back.
No matter if they're sick
or tired
or hungry.

Only ten percent
born this year
will see another spring.

No, if I get a second chance at life,
I'd choose to be me--

do it right this time.

Sanctuary

Each silken thread,
fragile alone,
grew in strength,
spun together
year after year.

Layer after layer,
a cocoon, in which
I safely hid my spark.

I'd visit every so often
in my dreams,
not daring to imagine
or venture forth--

fearful of discovery.

But then,
spark bursts into flame.
Silken walls
fight to hold back fire.

Beauty Born of Pain

Outside,
I unravel cords,
pack them away.

Death Lies Waiting

Heart quickens, breath slows—
I feel you inching closer,
not even trying
to be discreet.

A stalker, emboldened
by my fragility.

I'm not afraid,
I'm mad.
How dare you come
to take it all,
when I had so little to begin with?

Back off

You'll have me
eventually.

But not yet.

I'm not ready
for another selfish lover.

Can't Keep Up

information overload
moving too fast
I can't keep up

slow down
think things through
watch the wind in the trees

listen   to the silence

tread softly

in mind's tangled garden
fragrant flowers
poisonous and beautiful

surrounded by walls
built of sticks and stones

Poetry by Sally Quon

Not Ready

I’m not ready
to say goodbye
to soft summer mornings,
ponderosa pines
whispering lakes.

I’m not ready
to say goodbye
to leaves of rust and gold,
mushrooms in the forest,
air crisp enough to bite.

I’m not ready
to say goodbye
to soft snow falling silent,
Christmas mornings,
warm, wooly evenings.

Beauty Born of Pain

I'm not ready
to say goodbye
to spring's fresh wonders,
tender shoots,

light, laughing rain.

Circles

no beginning, no end
doomed to repeat
again, and again

I've had it with circles
give me a jagged line, a sharp edge
zigzag into tomorrow
where nothing is predictable

except

the rise and set of the sun
moon circling earth circling sun
turn of seasons
spinning wheel
life, death, rebirth

And Yet...

with soul-shattering speed
the world grew smaller each day.
betrayed by my body, sacrifices made,
a life
given over.

Is there no reward,
no golden days,
no god?

afraid.
    afraid to be alone,
to be a burden,
to take a step and falter.

how to see beyond
concessions made,
dreams
left to die on the clothesline.

in this battleground of
self-pity and blood-rage,
I gasp for air,
hunger for the simple joy
of movement,
out of gas,
out of luck,
out of hope.

and yet…

I rise,
the taste of joy, clear water on my lips.
words,
tangle and snarl,
splinter and separate,
fall into place,
shout out and rejoice.
and the world that grew small

breaks open.

part four:

RECOVERY

Wind

I heard the
wind
rustling in the pines.
Turned my face
to the sky,
tasting joy.

Poetry by Sally Quon

Morning in Rose Valley

Beside me
the grey-green pond

laughed

in the morning
light.

Quietly I sat,
while birds all around
called out to one another.

Stranger! Stranger!

and hid among the reeds.
Please
I thought out loud,

I only want to look at you.

Eventually they
forgot
I was there and one
hopped out onto a log
where we looked

at one another.

Here

in the heart of the forest,
where the silence is thunderous,
and the deep green rises to block out the sun.

Where the Western Wood Lilies that blanket the forest floor
shine with secret light.

Where the gods would choose
to take their morning walk
if they were of this world.

Where my mind
can steep in the stillness.

Here.

Ashes to Ashes

deep
within the heart of the cone
lies the seed
of the lodgepole pine
it's serotinous coat
deliberate
in its purpose
rebirth not possible
without sacrifice
soul released by fire

August

winding mountain road
dust in the darkness
new moon rising
nexus of night
beyond moss-covered canyon walls
to battle-scarred ground
remnants of last years burn
wind   whistling over rocky ground
shivering in the grass
we lay in
silence
as stars
fell from the sky
unhindered
by the dreams
of mortals
or pain of love

Sunlight

Sunlight drips like honey
from the trees.

The taste of euphoria
follows the wind.
A sky the colour of

forgiveness, and I –

I fall
into the impossible
intangible

morning.

Of the Morning

she rises
from her forest bed,
cajoling birds
into song.
sends her voice

over fields
of dusty gold,
coaxing coyotes

home to den.

spills across mountain passes,
where the sure-footed
goats clamber and fret.
falls upon the ocean

like mist

on the roses.

Texture, at the Edge of the World

patterns in the sand
        water-rippled
                wind-tossed
slip through my fingers like silk

patterns in the sky
        wind-rippled
                water-bloated
        light and airy
dark and stormy
shift and move like the rising tide

bark beneath my fingers
        Arbutus, cool and smooth
                Sitka spruce, thin and scaly
Cedar, sticky, sweet

leaves and needles, moss and salt
fragrance on a sea breeze

Poetry by Sally Quon

Forest

Take a deep breath.
Imagine
the wolf-wizened, gnarled

guardians

hanging their fairy lights,
inviting streams to dance.
A cacophony of sound

roaring through the consciousness
of sea-green tissue paper moss

dripping from branches,

falling over glacier-carved valleys and
bluebird breached cliffs of shale.

Take a deep breath.   What

is that smell?

Emily Carr

I wish I could be Emily Carr
live my life
unafraid
rejecting the norm
for the sake of my art

I want my life to spill onto the canvas
fierce with color
bold and spirit-strong

I want the pulse of the forest
to flow through me
and wander Haida Gwaii
memorizing the faded poles
until they crumble at last
to dust

I want a garden
wild and sweet
and a monkey who wears dresses
sewn
by my own two hands

Rain Dance

heat waves rising rippling air

ground shaking dance of
gathering storm clouds

deep the grey burgeoning wind

howling   cast out over dusty
fallow fields   birds

surge upward   spin   riding

currents that shift and flow
beckoning skyward she reaches out

touches thunder   soon

rain will come

After the Storm

grey sky gull morning
still water silent shore
storm-thrown clatter of debris

a perfect line in the sand

here now a man
with a bucket and a rake
scoop and scratch

scratch scratch scoop
line

interrupted

Poetry by Sally Quon

The Way

dimples in the sand
unfold
to water's edge

bits of wood scattered by wind
and wave

the scent of lake-weed rising

touching down   a gull
stretches a long
yellow leg

head cocked
he stoops to drink

takes flight

leaving behind a feather
tracks in the sand

the feather doesn't have to justify
its actions

it just falls

Lake-Walk

I walk out into the lake,
toward the buoy, far from shore.

Into the stillness of the morning.

The sun is warm on my shoulders,
the water sparkles in its light.
The bottom is silt and softness, and
the world – strangely silent.

I reach the buoy and turn,
startled to see the eddies
created by my presence.

Daydreams

Sunlight,
this beach.
Afternoon flows,
waves meet shore,
wind touches lips.
Daydreams
in aqua-marine.

Celebration

Silver wings in a
storm-blue sky

dip

to the horizon and

rise,

like the sun.

Spider

Spider,
spin your web for me.
Fold me in silken cords,
hammock-like
beneath the stars.

Swing me out over water,
feel the rush,
mother's blood,
warmth of womb,

beating heart.

Gird me to the earth,
silver strands
lissome in the wind.
Let me climb,
quench my thirst
on sun-speckled dew
and truth of morning.

Burn-scape

Fireweed, graminoids,
mushrooms and morels –

seed of a lodgepole pine.

Black-backed woodpeckers that nest
in the burned-out hollows.

Fire-following beetles and the
bats that follow them –

all waiting
for the lightning strike,
for the light

of a nascent flame.

Fish

End of the dock
same four chairs
there last week
        there last month

every season but winter
when they move out onto the ice
same four chairs
same four old men

grunting
"morning"
they sit in comfortable silence
unwrapping sandwiches from their buckets
when the sun reaches noon

a tug on the line
all turn to watch the prize reeled in

goldfish, descended from someone's discarded pet

turning back to their rods
they dream the same dream
of something better

Seasons Turn

The signs are here for all to see –
scattered leaf and sleepy tree.
Colder nights are just one tell
of summer's ebb and autumn's swell.
The hurried harvest of the grain,
the changing wind, the coming rain.
Orion rising in the night,
wild geese in southward flight.
The cheerful Robin's parting song –
and thistledown.

These Things

These things I will miss
when autumn comes no more –

Mustard-yellow leaves against a cerulean sky.
The dusty-moist fragrance of grain at harvest.

The low, golden glow of afternoon in late September.

The wild elk's haunting call to battle.
Watercolour days and painted sky nights –

These things, I will miss.

Imagine*

Imagine a star
falling from the heavens,
slicing through the atmosphere,
breaking up, burning free.
Punching a hole through your roof.
Coming to rest
on the pillow, next to your head.

Now,
moment by moment,
remind yourself
how lucky you are

to be here,
to breathe freely and
to wake each day
knowing the sun will also rise.

Steep yourself in gratitude
before the next star falls.

*In Response to "Meteorite Crashes Through Ceiling and Lands on Woman's Bed," *New York Times*, 2021.

Winter Morning

Pale sun rises
in a dove-grey sky.
Mountains,

a whisper

in the distance.
Ice fog clings
to every branch,
to every breath.

Quiet,

the music of morning.

19 Reasons To Keep Living

fragrance of morning
mock-orange blossoms
cascade down canyon walls
rain fattened clouds
smoky grey

drums, drums
rhythm of heartbeat
thunder in the sky

bittersweet longing
call of the loon
sweet kiss of rain
brushing skin

water and willow
on an episodic wind
wet grass
in the aftermath of storm

Poetry by Sally Quon

bird-song, chorus of frog, coyote calling
silent mind

slant of evening sunlight, falling in the forest
low, golden glow
dusty shadows shifting

moon-rise, star-shine
stillness of night
emerald ribbons
ripple midnight sky

predawn light of cobalt blue
earth and sky rising

the inevitable dawn

Triptych – The Kootenays

i.

How do you capture
the taste of a mountain stream
falling?

Iridescent mist
rising in the light

A crystal kiss on sun-laboured lips

Wings of a dragonfly

ii.

How do you capture
the sound of the wind?

Silence between spaces
when leaves are still

There is a honeybee
with a broken wing
listening to the ground

My footsteps,
thunder

iii.
How do you capture
the scent of a pine?

Sap-heavy hues
glowing verdant

Feathered fronds of delicate needles

Ballerinas practicing plies
in the breeze

One More Mountain Sunrise

One more mountain sunrise,
golden light, clouds of
peach and lilac.

The forest calls –
I answer.
Road dust and moss,
pinecones and birdsong.

I was going to write a poem for you.

Instead, I chose
one more mountain sunrise.

Poetry by Sally Quon

Cascade

emerging from a condo chrysalis
to a cabin in the woods
where water
tumbles, froths
wispy-white and olive brown
raucous laughter
crushing restless mind

mourning cloaks chase each other and the breeze
cottonwood fluff floating

sunlight moves over pools
unwrapping each new facet like a gift
and even the shadows are filled with color

American dippers fly the face of the falls
perch on boulders, bob and dive

all around the water flows

paths, once divergent
coalesce into one

a first step
tentative, hopeful

Acknowledgements

Just Thinking – Voicing Suicide: A Poetry Anthology, edited by Daniel Scott, Ekstasis Editions, 2020

Pieces – Quills Canadian Poetry, 2023

On the Farm – Hearthbeat, Hidden Brook Press, 2020

Wild Horses – Ethelzine Issue 10, 2022

Sharon – Canadian Stories 10th Contest Magazine, 2018

The Matriarch – Poetry Pause, The League of Canadian Poets, 2022

Eyes of a Child – Buddy Breathing, a blog by Lesley-Anne Evans, 2021

Gold – Dr. William Henry Drummond Poetry Contest Anthology, 2020

Photograph – Poetry Pause, The League of Canadian Poets, 2022

Lake (third section of the poem Water) – Dribbles, Drabbles, and Postcards, edited by Darcy Nybo, 2022

Cobwebs – The Abstract of Time Anthology, The Rudderless Mariner, 2021

Inevitable – Quills Canadian Poetry Magazine, 2023

Living Rough – Word City Literary Journal, 2022

Colour – Quills Canadian Poetry Magazine, 2023

Night – Oyedrum On-line, 2022

Death Lies Waiting – Quills Canadian Poetry Magazine, 2023

And Yet… - Where Flowers Bloom, Red Penguin Books, 2022

Wind – Pocket Lint, Third Edition by Warren Dean Fulton, 2021

Morning in Rose Valley – The Old Veranda Swing, Poetry Institute of Canada, 2018

Here – The Tree Journal, Tiny Seeds Literary Journal, 2019, Reprinted (with edits) in Better Left

Standing, edited by Christina Lowther, Caitlin Press, 2022

August – Wine Country Writer's Festival Contest Anthology, 2021

Of the Morning – Sunbeams: Anthology of the Joan Ramsayer Memorial Poetry Contest, 2019

Daydreams – Planet Earth Poetry on Instagram, 2022

Celebration – The Ontario Poetry Society Ultra Short Poem Contest Anthology, 2019

Spider – Tiny Seeds Literary Journal On-line, 2020

Burn-scape – Tiny Seeds Literary Journal On-line, 2020

Season's Turn – the leaves fall anthology, Red Penguin Books, 2021

Imagine – Lothlorien Journal On-line, 2022

19 Reasons to Keep on Living – Fresh Voices 2022, The League of Canadian Poets, 2021

One More Mountain Sunrise – Vallum Magazine Blog, 2021

Cascade – Central Texas Writer's Society Nature Anthology, 2021, Reprinted in Coming Out of

Isolation: Poems on Resilience, Triumph, and Hope, Edited by Christopher Okemwa,

Verlag Expeditonen, 2022

Sorry, Not Sorry – Dear You, Red Penguin Books, 2023

Broken – Dear You, Red Penguin Books, 2023

Questions – Dear You, Red Penguin Books, 2023

Things I Will Not Do Today – Dear You, Red Penguin Books, 2023

www.ingramcontent.com/pod-product-compliance
Lightning Source LLC
LaVergne TN
LVHW090122160826
845673LV00015B/528

* 9 7 8 1 9 9 0 3 8 9 3 0 6 *